Adrian Peterson

by Mari Schuh

Consultant: Barry Wilner
AP Football Writer

BEARPORT
PUBLISHING

New York, New York

Credits

Cover and Title Page, © Genevieve Ross/AP Images and David Stluka/AP Images; 4, © fotokik_dot_com/Shutterstock Images; 5 © Bryan C. Singer/Icon SMI; 6, © Nati Harnik/ AP Images; 7, © Bryan C. Singer/Icon SMI; 8, © Ffooter/Shutterstock Images; 9, © Chris McGrath/Getty Images; 10, © Bryan C. Singer/Icon SMI; 11, © AJ Mansour; 12, © Seth Poppel/Yearbook Library; 13, © iosphotos/Newscom; 14, © David Branch, Tyler Morning Telegraph/AP Images; 15, © J.P. Wilson/Icon SMI; 16, © Bryan C. Singer/Icon SMI; 17, © Cliff Welch/Icon SMI; 18, © Kirk Aeder/Icon SMI; 19, © Larry Smith/Icon SMI; 20, © Bryan C. Singer/Icon SMI; 21, © Tom Croke/Icon SMI; 22, © Larry Smith/Icon SMI.

Publisher: Kenn Goin
Editorial Director: Adam Siegel
Senior Editor: Joyce Tavolacci
Creative Director: Spencer Brinker
Photo Researcher: Arnold Ringstad
Design: Emily Love

Library of Congress Cataloging-in-Publication Data

Schuh, Mari.
  Adrian Peterson / by Mari Schuh.
      p. cm. — (Football stars up close)
  Includes bibliographical references and index.
  ISBN 978-1-61772-718-4 (library binding) — ISBN 1-61772-718-0 (library binding)
  1. Peterson, Adrian—Juvenile literature. 2. Football players—United States—Biography—Juvenile literature. I. Title.
  GV939.P477S58 2013
  796.332092—dc23
  [B]
                                    2012035406

For more information, write to Bearport Publishing Company, Inc., 45 West 21st Street, Suite 3B, New York, New York 10010. Printed in the United States of America.

10 9 8 7 6 5 4 3 2 1

Contents

Touchdown Time

It was November 4, 2007. The Minnesota Vikings lined up against the San Diego Chargers. The Vikings' quarterback handed the football to Adrian Peterson. Adrian gripped the ball tightly and **sprinted** down the field. The Chargers tried to **tackle** him, but Adrian was too fast and strong. Before the Chargers knew it, Adrian was in the **end zone**. He had scored a 46-yard (42 m) **touchdown**!

The Metrodome in downtown Minneapolis, where Adrian made his touchdown

The Vikings play in Minneapolis, Minnesota. Their stadium, which was built in 1982, is called the Metrodome.

Adrian sprints past Chargers players in the November 2007 game.

Record-Breaking Running Back

The Vikings went on to beat the Chargers 35–17. It was a record-breaking game for Adrian. He ran for 296 yards (271 m), setting an **NFL** record. No **running back** had ever run that many yards in one game before. Even more amazing, Adrian was a rookie. It was just his eighth game in the NFL.

Adrian meets with young fans in 2007.

Adrian dodges a tackle during the game against the Chargers.

A rookie is a player in his or her first year in a sport. Adrian averaged almost 96 yards (88 m) per game in his rookie year.

A Family of Athletes

Adrian was born on March 21, 1985, in Palestine, Texas. He grew up in a family of athletes. His dad played basketball in college. His mom was a star **sprinter**. One of his uncles was an NFL running back. Adrian wanted to be an athlete too. He started playing football when he was only seven years old.

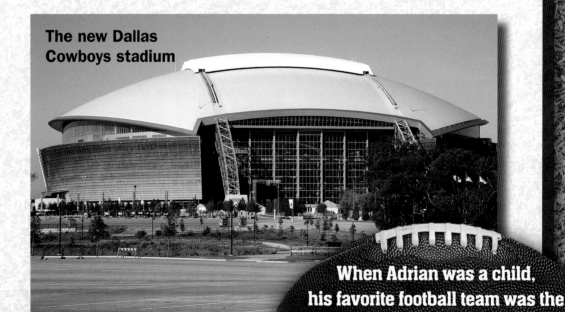

The new Dallas Cowboys stadium

When Adrian was a child, his favorite football team was the Dallas Cowboys. The Cowboys play in Texas. The team built a huge new stadium in 2009.

Adrian's mom and dad were very proud of him when he became an NFL player.

Working Out

When he became older, Adrian wanted to lift weights to build up his muscles. However, his family could not afford to buy weights. So he found other ways to work out. Adrian filled old water jugs with sand or water and dragged them behind him as he ran. Adrian also ran up and down steep hills. All of these activities helped make him a more powerful athlete.

Adrian had to work hard to become so strong and fast.

Adrian lifts weights to stay strong.

As a young boy, Adrian got the nickname A.D., which stands for All Day. His mom and dad gave him the nickname because Adrian's energy lasted all day long.

High School Star

Adrian played football as a running back at Palestine High School during his junior and senior years. In 2003, when he was a senior, he scored an unbelievable 32 touchdowns! That year, Adrian was named one of the top high school football players in the United States.

Adrian's yearbook picture from his junior year of high school

Adrian sprints to the finish line in high school.

In high school, Adrian also played basketball and ran races. He was a sprinter, just like his mother had been.

13

College Days

Many colleges wanted Adrian to play football for them. He chose the University of Oklahoma. For three years, he used his power and speed to run for an amazing total of 4,045 yards (3,699 m)! Sadly, Adrian broke his collarbone during his junior year in 2006. As a result, he missed the last seven games of the season.

Adrian (right) and his mom (left) and brother (center) when he told reporters that he would be playing for the University of Oklahoma

Adrian (center) runs with the ball in a 2006 game against Iowa State.

In 2004, his first year playing college football, Adrian was runner-up for the **Heisman Trophy.**

Turning Pro

Adrian chose to skip his senior year of college and play in the NFL. During the 2007 NFL **draft**, the Minnesota Vikings picked Adrian. He signed a **contract** to play for the Vikings for six years. Adrian was excited to show the team what he could do.

Adrian sprints with the ball during practice the summer before his first NFL season.

In Adrian's 2007 contract, the Vikings agreed to pay him more than $40 million over six years.

Adrian holds up his new jersey after being picked by the Vikings in the 2007 NFL draft.

Record Breaker

Adrian soon showed everyone that he was a star player. He began breaking records in his NFL rookie year. He set a Vikings record with an average of 5.6 yards (5.1 m) each time he ran with the ball. Adrian also had the most **rushing yards** per game of any player in the NFL. He ran a total of 1,341 yards (1,226 m) that season. The next season, in 2008, he rushed for 1,760 yards (1,609 m).

Adrian carries the ball in the 2008 Pro Bowl.

Adrian was picked for the NFL Pro Bowl every year from 2008 to 2011.

Adrian celebrates after scoring a touchdown in a 2007 game against the Dallas Cowboys.

Best in the League

Adrian dazzled Vikings fans with his strength and speed. In 2011, he agreed to play for the team for seven more years. Unfortunately, he hurt his left knee in a game later that year. As a result, Adrian played only 12 games that season. However, he began working hard to build his strength back in order to play again in 2012. After all, as his nickname makes clear, A.D. is one of the hardest working players in football.

Adrian puts on his helmet in 2012 before his first game after his knee injury.

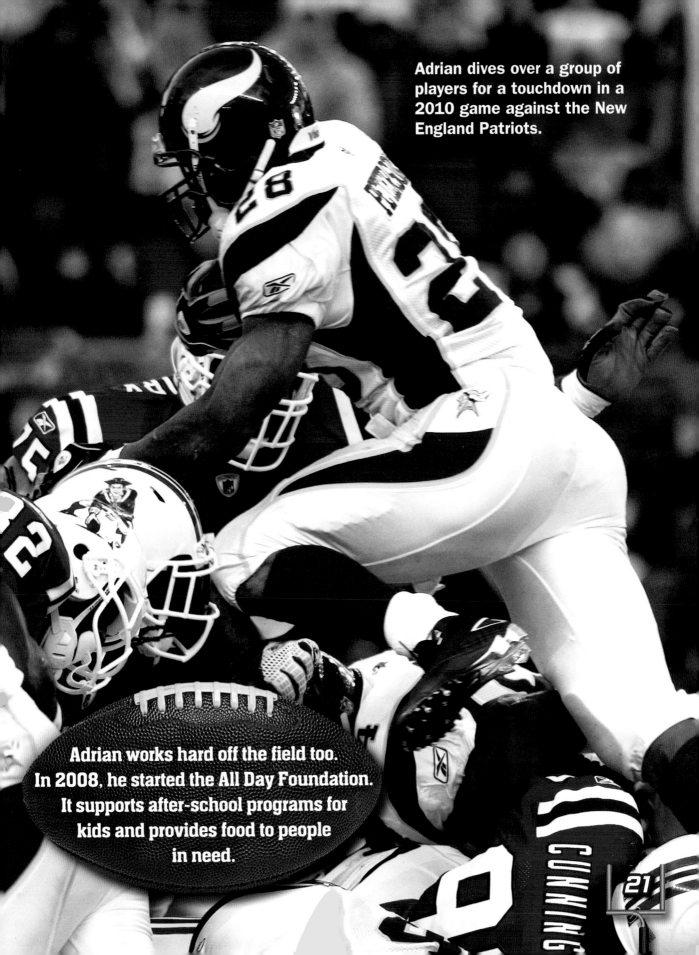

Adrian dives over a group of players for a touchdown in a 2010 game against the New England Patriots.

Adrian works hard off the field too. In 2008, he started the All Day Foundation. It supports after-school programs for kids and provides food to people in need.

Adrian's Life and Career

★ **March 21, 1985**   Adrian Peterson is born in Palestine, Texas.

★ **1992**   At age seven, Adrian starts to play football.

★ **2003**   Adrian scores 32 touchdowns during his senior year at Palestine High School.

★ **2004**   Adrian is runner-up for the Heisman Trophy.

★ **2006**   Adrian breaks his collarbone during his junior year at the University of Oklahoma.

★ **2007**   The Minnesota Vikings select Adrian during the NFL draft.

★ **2008**   Adrian starts the All Day Foundation to help people in need.

★ **2008–2011**   Adrian is chosen for the NFL Pro Bowl each year.

★ **2011**   Adrian agrees to play seven more years for the Vikings.

★ **2011–2012**   Adrian injures his left knee, cutting his season short, and then returns to the Vikings.

22

Glossary

contract (KON-trakt)
a written agreement between people or companies that tells how much one of them will be paid to perform a certain job

draft (DRAFT)
an event in which NFL teams take turns choosing college players to play for them

end zone (END ZOHN)
the area at either end of a football field where touchdowns are scored

Heisman Trophy
(HIGHZ-man TROH-fee)
an award given to the best college football player in the country

NFL (EN-EFF-ELL)
letters standing for the *National Football League*, which includes 32 teams

Pro Bowl (PROH BOHL)
the NFL's all-star game that is for the season's best NFL players

running back (RUN-ing BAK)
a football player who carries the ball on running plays

rushing yards (RUHSH-ing YARDZ)
yards gained on plays in which a player runs with the ball

sprinted (SPRINT-id)
ran at top speed for a short distance

sprinter (SPRINT-ur)
a person who runs short, fast races

tackle (TAK-uhl)
to grab players from the other team and drag or knock them to the ground

touchdown (TUHCH-doun)
a score of six points, made by getting the football across the other team's goal line

Index

Bibliography

Associated Press. "Peterson Rushes into Record Book with 296
Yards." *The New York Times* (November 5, 2007).

Official Site of the Minnesota Vikings: www.vikings.com

Official Site of the NFL: www.NFL.com

Read More

Frisch, Aaron. *Adrian Peterson (The Big Time).* Mankato, MN:
Creative Education (2013).

Gitlin, Marty. *Adrian Peterson: Record-Setting Running Back
(Playmakers).* Minneapolis, MN: ABDO (2012).

Savage, Jeff. *Adrian Peterson (Amazing Athletes).* Minneapolis, MN:
Lerner (2011).

Learn More Online

To learn more about Adrian Peterson, visit
www.bearportpublishing.com/FootballStarsUpClose